The Little
Beige Book of
Quotations

Selected and edited

by Paul Kocak

Quote Victoria,
Enjoy unquote.
Paul Kocak

ISBN: 9798393717667 (paperback)

Interior layout, composition, and cover design by **ebookpbook**.

Also by Paul Kocak

To librarians everywhere

Introduction

Words, words, words. *Other* people's words, words, words. What's the point of a book like this? As with *The Dog-Eared Book of Dog-Eared Quotations,* you are invited to give the words here new life. After all, quotations should be — well — quoted! Try them out as conversation starters (or enders). Use these nuggets as a speaker or a writer. A quotation is a brilliant way to start a meeting, giving it a focus and an anchor. It's also valuable as an epigraph or as a writing prompt. Many great speeches build on, or alter, a famous quotation. Speaking of "alter," quotations are notorious for modifications that alter the original wording; they morph. Quotations also are a hotbed of misattribution. The provenance and correctness of any quotation is a scholar's mine field. But I am not a scholar and this does not claim to be a scholarly work. Nevertheless, I have been diligent in seeking to render each quotation accurately. As for attributions, I correct the record if new information has arisen among the quoters' community. I confess to being inconsistent in identifying quotation sources. Sometimes I lacked solid evidence; other times, I chose to limit how far to follow a tenuous source thread.

Most quotations here are modern, meaning from 1900 onward. I have taken slight liberties with capitalization, punctuation, spacing, or line breaks when needed to fashion a stand-alone set of words. Naturally, the start or finish of any quotation involves editorial discretion. Good wordsmith detectives can spot minuscule shifts from the original — which undoubtedly unhinges scholars and researchers. For pithiness, in some cases, I started the selected quotation after "and" or "but" found in the original text. I have converted British spellings to American spellings for consistency. In all instances, I have labored to avoid doctoring the quotes or altering them to serve my purposes. I have sought to stay true to the original text or spoken words, but recognize that by the nature of what I am doing words are taken out of context.

All quotations are taken out of context to some degree. They are severed from their original environment. But we don't speak with footnotes. Quotations need to be quotable on their own if they are to survive. As radical as it might seem, I invite you to create new contexts for the words jostling here. Happy quoting!

— Paul Kocak

Table of contents

1

THE PAST

The past is never dead. It's not even past.

William Faulkner

All things must pass.

George Harrison

Every human being is an archeological site.

Lucy Sante

The power of the visible is the invisible.

Marianne Moore

The world is full of mostly invisible things.

Howard Nemerov

Lend me the stone strength of the past and I will lend you /
The wings of the future, for I have them.

Robinson Jeffers

If you're strong enough, there *are* no precedents.

F. Scott Fitzgerald

Your past is just a story. And once you realize this, it has
no power over you.

Chuck Palahniuk

Understanding the past requires pretending that you
don't know the present.

Paul Fussell

It is difficult at times to repress the thought that history
is about as instructive as an abattoir.

Seamus Heaney

You cannot not know history.

Philip Johnson

Life is simply what our feelings do to us.

Honoré de Balzac

Life is like an overlong drama through which we sit being
nagged by the vague memories of having read the reviews.

John Updike

The sex act cruelly mimics history's decline and fall.

Camille Paglia

But it's the covering of the tracks that always gets you in the end.

Jackson Lamb, *Slow Horses*

There is no trap so deadly as the trap you set for yourself.

Raymond Chandler

Sometimes the only way to work out why a trap has been set is to walk into it.

Jackson Lamb, *Slow Horses*

The only reason people want to be masters of the future is to change the past.

Milan Kundera

The moment of change is the only poem.

Adrienne Rich

Rationality will not save us.

Robert S. McNamara

Holding on is believing that there's only a past; letting go is knowing that there's a future.

Daphne Rose Kingma

The future is always beginning now.

Mark Strand

There is always one moment in childhood when the door opens and lets the future in.

Graham Greene

The past is always tense and the future, perfect.

Zadie Smith, *White Teeth*

There is no bad time for good news.

Stephen King

The heart's memory eliminates the bad and magnifies the good.

Gabriel García Márquez

Have you decided yet what historical moment you would have most like to have witnessed with your own eyes and ears?

Padgett Powell

The past has revealed to me the structure of the future.

Pierre Teilhard de Chardin

Do you know anyone who would — secretly, sincerely, in his innermost self — *really* prefer to return to childhood?

Anita Desai

Nostalgia isn't what it used to be.

Peter De Vries

Each had his past shut in him like the leaves of a book known to him by heart; and his friends could only read the title.

Virginia Woolf

We both know what memories can bring / They bring diamonds and rust.

Joan Baez

This was supposed to happen, because that's what did happen.

Pam Benson

Life could not continue without throwing the past into the past, liberating the present from its burden

Paul Tillich

When does remembering the past start to ruin the future?

Robert Icke

After loving you so much, can I forget / you for eternity, and have no other choice?

Robert Lowell

History and memory share events; that is, they share time and space. Every Moment is two moments.

Anne Michaels

We learn from history that we do not learn from history.

Georg Hegel

History justifies whatever we want it to. It teaches absolutely nothing, for it contains everything and gives examples of everything.

Paul Valéry

History is not interesting — what is interesting is the anecdote.

Karl Lagerfeld

Longing on a large scale is what makes history.

Don De Lillo

In truth, history is written by the romantics, as stories are won by storytellers.

Adam Gopnik

The difference between hope and despair is a different way of telling stories from the same facts.

Alain de Botton

I think it helps to have some kind of little story, don't you?

David Sedaris

Look, sometimes the truth can ruin a perfectly good story.
Rebecca Welton, *Ted Lasso*

Aesthetes may lose the local battle; they usually win the historical war.

Adam Gopnik

Anyone who can spin lore and chivalry, higher calling and mystic purpose, from the ugliness of warfare can claim the tale, even in defeat.

Adam Gopnik

You can be a museum or you can be modern, but you can't be both.

Gertrude Stein

If you understood everything I said, you'd be me.

Miles Davis

Whatever they thought they'd understood was not wrong but irrelevant.

Rumaan Alam

Everything's weird if you look long enough.

Sam Lipsyte

The trouble with sins and sorrows . . . is that in time they become boring, even to the sorrowing sinner.

Benjamin Black, *Elegy for April*

There's only one real sin, and that is to persuade oneself that the second-best is anything but the second-best.

Doris Lessing

I don't think you can ever do your best. Doing your best is a process of trying to do your best.

Townes Van Zandt

To me comfort is like the wrong memory at the wrong place or time: if one is lonely one prefers discomfort.

Graham Greene

Loneliness can be conquered only by those who can bear solitude.

Paul Tillich

Many people misjudge the permanent effect of sorrow and their capacity to live in the past.

Ivy Compton-Burnett

Write your sad times in sand; write your good times in stone.

George Bernard Shaw

The sadness was always there, an underground cascade.

Mona Simpson

The past rests, breathing faintly in the darkness.

Scott Spencer

. . . the past wastes no time becoming the past . . .

Benjamin Black, *Elegy for April*

So we beat on, boats against the current, borne back ceaselessly into the past.

F. Scott Fitzgerald

When you take a flower in your hand and really look at it, it's your world for the moment. I want to give that world to someone else.

Georgia O'Keeffe

I was a thought in the shape / Of a spring flower.

Joy Harjo, "An Ordinary Morning"

I don't want to end up simply having visited this world.

Mary Oliver

I'd like to know when it's coming / Just a little time to prepare / When the voice of midnight comes / I hope you will be there.

Slaid Cleaves

— our memory is outside ourselves, in a rainy breath of time

Annie Ernaux

The hum in our ears is our own history, and that hum never goes away.

Carol Shields

The struggle against power is the struggle of memory against forgetting.

Milan Kundera

Nobody's as powerful as we make them out to be.

Alice Walker

How we lived, and lived, and lived / And loved our living.

Joy Harjo

. . . how miraculous it is to exist. To live beyond survival. To be alive / twice and thrice, and countless times to find one with and within another.

Paul Tran

I was in love with the whole world and all that lived in its rainy arms.

Louise Erdrich

Too many lives are needed to make just one.

Eugenio Montale

How we spend our days is, of course, how we spend our lives.

Annie Dillard

Only anachronism has a chance to outlast the epoch.

Franz Werfel

Memory is a skilled seducer.

Cristina García

Memory believes before knowing remembers.

William Faulkner

Like a dream, / Whatever I enjoy / Will become a memory; / The past is not revisited.

Shantideva

The past is a foreign country: they do things differently there.

L.P. Hartley

Unhappy is the land that needs a hero.

Bertolt Brecht

Imagination, like memory, can transform lies to truths.

Cristina García

He entered the territory of lies without a passport for return.

Graham Greene

A lie ain't a side of a story. It's just a lie.

Terry Hanning, *The Wire*

A man who will lie for me will lie to me.

Arthur Morgan

There is always a mirror, and you are never alone when you look in one.

Joseph O'Connor

Mirrors are the doors through which Death comes and goes.

Jean Cocteau

The past is a hall of mirrors, not of statues.

Julia Glass

Beauty is nothing but the beginning of terror.

Rainer Maria Rilke

In such ugly times, the only true protest is beauty."

Phil Ochs

Beauty is the final spasm of a rigorous inquisitorial process. Every rose grows in a prison.

Salvador Dali

Magnificent desolation.

Buzz Aldrin [said during first moon walk]

Don't send me no more letters, no, not unless you mail them from Desolation Row.

Bob Dylan

Of almost everything we retained little beyond a word, detail or name that would later make us say, . . . "I remember."

Annie Ernaux

. . . there begin to be fissures / in what we remember, / and within a year or two, / the facts break apart / . . . and the past has become / a new world.

Ted Kooser

I dreamt the past was never past redeeming.

Richard Wilbur

Someday maybe I'll remember to forget.

Bob Dylan

Time robs us and robs us and when we beg for mercy, it robs us some more.

Michael Cunningham

Time is dead as long as it is being clicked off by little wheels; only when the clock stops does time come to life.

William Faulkner

Everything that has been will be, everything that will be is, everything that will be has been.

Eugène Ionesco

2

THE PRESENT

Let the wild rumpus start!

Maurice Sendak

That Was Then, This Is Now

S. E. Hinton

There is less in this than meets the eye.

Tallulah Bankhead

Forever is composed of nows.

Emily Dickinson

What would it be like if I could accept life — accept this moment — exactly as it is?

Tara Brach

I am the only guinea pig I have.

R. Buckminster Fuller

What am I without you?

Jiayang Fan

Tell me, what is it you plan to do with your one wild and precious life?

Mary Oliver

What a wonderful life I've had! I only wish I'd realized it sooner.

Sidonie-Gabrielle Colette

I never saw a wild thing / Sorry for itself.

D. H. Lawrence

If the only prayer you ever say in your entire life is thank you, it will be enough.

Meister Eckhart

If I could pray, I'd have one hand of shadow / and one of light, I'd be a folded thing, a voice / born on wings. . .

Bob Hicok

If we want things to stay as they are, things will have to change.

Giuseppe di Lampedusa

It is not the strongest spider that survives . . . but the one most responsive to change.

Charles Darwin

You are what you do, not what you say you'll do.

Carl Jung

So what. Now what?

Linda Cliatt-Wayman

My impulse to fall into addiction was a reminder of how close to destruction I reside.

Russell Brand

When the beginnings of self-destruction enter the heart it seems no bigger than a grain of sand.

John Cheever

No snowflake in an avalanche ever feels responsible.

Stanislaw J. Lec

I was like, "You're doing this wrong. You're afraid to be you, and you've gotten everything you wanted."

Dax Shepard

Don't make jokes that require research.

Brian Morton

What is that unforgettable line?

Samuel Beckett

The itch of a lost quotation in a book you cannot find.

Hannah Sullivan

One has to secrete a jelly in which to slip quotations down people's throats and one always secretes too much jelly.

Virginia Woolf

It's a good thing for an uneducated man to read books of quotations.

Winston Churchill

People who like quotes love meaningless generalizations.

Graham Greene

Life itself is a quotation.

Jorge Luis Borges

Of course you don't like all the aphorisms. I don't like all of you.

Don Paterson

It is invariably oneself that one collects.

Jean Baudrillard

It's better to be quotable than to be honest.

Tom Stoppard

All cruel people describe themselves as paragons of frankness.

Tennessee Williams

Sometimes it seems the only accomplishment my education ever bestowed on me, the ability to think in quotations.

Margaret Drabble

They dug each other's references and felt smarter in each other's presence.

Chris Kraus

I think one of my gifts is also one of my weaknesses, which is I have an antenna for other people.

Terry Gross

You've got to learn the no word.

Bruce Springsteen

You're not present because you're waiting for a punch. That's how I feel. I feel like I have my dukes up all day long looking for someone who's going to punch me, and here's the thing, no one ever punches me.

Judd Apatow

Get up, stand up, / Stand up for your rights.

Bob Marley

Get back up. Begin again.

Brené Brown

You never know how strong you are until being strong is the only choice you have.

Bob Marley

When you're right, be quiet.

Deeksha Joshi

Astound me. [*Étonne-moi.*]

Sergei Diaghilev

'Scuse me while I kiss the sky.

Jimi Hendrix

Here we are now, entertain us.

Kurt Cobain

To bring someone more than what he asks for, he has to ask for something in the first place.

Brian Morton

We are in great haste to construct a magnetic telegraph from Maine to Texas; but Maine and Texas, it may be, have nothing important to communicate.

Henry David Thoreau

It is completely unimportant. That is why it is so interesting.

Agatha Christie

It ain't braggin' if you can do it.

Dizzy Dean

Reality is that which when you stop believing in it, it doesn't go away.

Philip K. Dick

Reality had always been something of an unknown quantity to me.

Anna Kavan

I am invisible, understand, simply because people refuse to see me.

Ralph Ellison

I have never doubted the truth of signs.

Umberto Eco

A conspiracy is everything that ordinary life is not.

Don De Lillo

It doesn't matter if the cat is black or white as long as it catches mice.

Deng Xiaoping

One thing or another will happen. Then one thing or another will happen.

Glenn Close, quoting Mary Beth Hurt

No role is so well suited to philosophy as the one you happen to be in right now.

Marcus Aurelius

My great problem in life is that I do not really know what my role in life is. I must find one.

King Charles III

One does not sell the earth upon which the people walk.

Crazy Horse (Ta-Sunko-Witko)

Indeed, if Charles checked his privilege, there would be nothing left of him — just a crumpled pile of ermine and velvet, and a faint whiff of Eau Sauvage.

Rebecca Mead

It isn't easy to defend yourself without coming across as defensive.

Laura Miller

Bewildered, bewildered, you have no complaint. / You are what you are, and you ain't what you ain't.

John Prine

Even though you can't expect to defeat the absurdity of the world, you must make that attempt. That's morality, that's religion. That's art. That's life.

Phil Ochs

I believe there are crimes in life but no crimes in art.

Paul Schrader

I am an atheist still, thank God.

Luis Buñuel

God Was Here but He Left Early

Irwin Shaw

Any God I ever felt in church I brought in with me.

Alice Walker

There is no God and we are his prophets.

Cormac McCarthy

I am very much down to earth. Just not this earth.

Karl Lagerfeld

All I am is what I'm going after.

Lt. Vincent Hanna, *Heat*

One should never arrive in an unknown place at night, everything is undefined, every object is easily exaggerated.

Elena Ferrante, *The Lost Daughter*

Does anybody know my name, or recognize my face / I must have come from somewhere, but I can't recall the place.

Phil Ochs

Let us all be from somewhere.

Bob Hicok

You're still using your eyes to see the world, instead of adopting the proper skewed perspective of an egomaniac.

Nell Zink

There is no doubt about it, the modern thunderstorm no longer clears the air.

Jacques Barzun

...we're at the beginning of living in a time when you can't really keep secrets anymore.

Kristen V. Brown

The world keeps ending but new people too dumb to know it keep showing up as if the fun's just started.

John Updike

Rooting is in our blood; we take sides as we take breaths.

Janet Malcolm

The magic of a thing you'd normally see only from a distance disappears when you see it up close. But a new magic takes its place.

Rachel Kushner, "A King Alone"

Sometimes distance showed a thing most clearly.

Rumaan Alam

I am alone here in my own mind. / There is no map / And there is no road.

Anne Sexton

She belonged to no club and was a member of nothing in the world.

Carson McCullers

Making things is my favorite part of making things.

Angel Olsen

I'm just a child who's learned to impersonate an adult.

Michael Cunningham.

It is a good thing for an uneducated man to read books of quotations.

Winston Churchill

A successful book is not made of what is *in* it, but of what is left *out* of it.

Mark Twain

There is no such thing as a moral or an immoral book. Books are well written, or badly written. That is all.

Oscar Wilde

There is nothing like a good book to put you to sleep with the illusion that life is rich and meaningful.

Robert Penn Warren

People seldom read a book which is given to them.

Samuel Johnson

Thank God for books as an alternative to conversation.

W. H. Auden

What if we just went home and read books to each other?

Gary Shteyngart

Gods do not answer letters.

John Updike

In the dying world I come from quotation is a national vice. It used to be the classics, now it's lyric verse.

Evelyn Waugh

Life is slow suicide, unless you read.

Herman Wouk

Welcome to the desert of the ritual.

Louis Menand

I'm not my type.

> Morrissey, "Spent the Day in Bed"

The way you are is the way you have to be.

> Preston Sturges

The place you are right now, God circled on a map for you.

> Hafiz

The world being illusive, one must be deluded in some way if one is to triumph.

> William Butler Yeats

Look on every exit as being an entrance somewhere else.

> Tom Stoppard

People enter and exit the world; that's the real news.

> Carol Shields

The mind that is not baffled is not employed.

> Wendell Berry

He had a mind so fine that no idea could violate it.

> T. S. Eliot

Welcome to the world of reality — there is no audience. No one to applaud, to admire. No one to see you.

> David Foster Wallace, *Something to Do with Paying Attention*

I don't want to end up simply having visited this world.

Mary Oliver

How is it possible to have a *civil* war?

George Carlin

We must end this uncivil war.

Joe Biden

I have a fine sense of the ridiculous, but no sense of humor.

Edward Albee

Humor is a prelude to faith and / Laughter is the beginning of prayer.

Reinhold Niebuhr

Laughter is an instant vacation.

Milton Berle

Laughter is the sun that drives winter from the human face.

Victor Hugo

There is nothing more precious than laughter.

Frida Kahlo

There is one path in the world that none can walk but you.

Frederick Nietzsche

If you are intimidated by every rub, how will your mirror be polished?

Langston Hughes

There are two ways of spreading light, to be the candle and the mirror that reflects it.

Edith Wharton

It's always night, or we wouldn't need light.

Thelonious Monk

A Long Day's Journey into Night

Eugene O'Neill

The spectrum is an invitation: it asks us to join the rest of the world on a continuum of suffering.

Roy Richard Grinker

. . . when the unexpected suddenly occurs, there is nothing to do but wait

Annie Ernaux

. . . nothing's like it used to be, not even the future.

Rita Dove

Time plays like an accordion in the way it can stretch out and compress itself in a thousand melodic ways.

Julia Glass

Prediction is very difficult, especially about the future.

Niels Bohr

The future is the most expensive luxury in the world.

Thornton Wilder

Don't criticize yourself for whatever it is you're doing. Just notice what it is.

Pema Chödrön

One day or day one. You decide.

Paulo Coelho

Who has more power than a child?

Michael Cunningham

With digital technology, we drained reality dry.

Annie Ernaux

It is not our private yearnings but our public follies that finally define us.

Rachel Syme

We are what we pretend to be.

Kurt Vonnegut Jr.

The future is much like the present, only longer.

Dan Quisenberry

3

NOTHINGS & EVERYTHINGS

Nothing, capital N, exists, simultaneously with Everything, capital E.

Joan Konner

"Nothing" is the force / That renovates the World —

Emily Dickinson

Between grief and nothing I will take grief.

William Faulkner

Not everything that is faced can be changed, but nothing can be changed until it is faced.

James Baldwin

Much of spiritual life is self-acceptance, maybe all of it.
Jack Kornfield

Acceptance is usually more a matter of fatigue than anything else.
David Foster Wallace

I've never found a way / to hide my doing nothing / day after day.
W. S. Merwin

At first nothing will happen to us / and later on / it will happen to us again.
Leonard Cohen

Blessed be nothing.
Ralph Waldo Emerson

Some alien blessing / is on its way to us.
W. S. Merwin

To gain that which is worth having, it may be necessary to lose everything else.
Bernadette Devlin

The United States of Amnesia.
Gore Vidal

This is what history consists of. It's the sum total of all the things they aren't telling us.

Don De Lillo

It Can't Happen Here

Sinclair Lewis

Where, in a poem, is "here"?

Kamran Javadizadeh

There are fuckers and fuckees.

John Lennon

We see nothingness making the world iridescent, casting a shimmer over things.

Jean-Paul Sartre

The feelings of my smallness and my nothingness always kept me good company.

Pope John XXIII

Nothing is our own. We begin the world as anagrams of our antecedents.

Maggie O'Farrell, *The Vanishing Act of Esmé Lennox*

What people forget is a journey to nowhere starts with a single step, too.

Chuck Palahniuk

America I've given you all and now I'm nothing.
Allen Ginsberg

Democracy is the fig leaf of elitism.
Florence King

The whole peninsula of Florida was weighted down with regret. Everyone had left behind a real life.
Cynthia Ozick

Life for me ain't been no crystal stair.
Langston Hughes

Been Down So Long It Looks Like Up to Me
Richard Fariña

There is a here here.
Joan Konner

When one does nothing, one believes oneself responsible for everything.
Jean-Paul Sartre

I am deeply superficial.
Ava Gardner

When people call you intelligent it is almost always because they agree with you. Otherwise they call you arrogant.
Nassim Nicholas Taleb

All great truths begin as blasphemies.

George Bernard Shaw

The truth will set you free. But not until it is finished with you.

David Foster Wallace

Never think you've seen the last of anything.

Eudora Welty

The sad truth of the matter is that most evil is done by people who never mind up their minds to be or do either evil or good.

Hannah Arendt

Evil is unspectacular and always human, / And shares our bed and eats at our own table.

W. H. Auden

Between two evils, I always pick the one I never tried before.

Mae West

One cannot be precise and still be pure.

Marc Chagall

I would like to be the air that inhabits you for a moment only. I would like to be that unnoticed and that necessary.

Margaret Atwood

Always remember that you are absolutely unique. Just like everyone else.

Margaret Mead

All charming people have something to conceal, usually their total dependence on the appreciation of others.

Cyril Connolly

When a man tells you that he got rich through hard work, ask him: "Whose?"

Don Marquis

One never knows where the velocity of bad feeling comes from, how it advances.

Elena Ferrante

The best way out is always through.

Robert Frost

What is a rebel? A man who says no.

Albert Camus

No, Thursday's out. How about never — is never good for you?

Robert Mankoff

Everybody hates me because I'm universally liked.

Peter De Vries

Everybody does have a book in them, but in most cases that's where it should stay.

Christopher Hitchens

A bad book is as much of a labor to write as a good one; it comes as sincerely from the author's soul.

Aldous Huxley

Lofty souls are always inclined to make a virtue of misfortune.

Honoré de Balzac

Nothing in the universe resembles God more than silence.

Meister Eckhart

I was the accuser, God the accused. My eyes were open and I was alone — terribly alone in a world without God and without man.

Elie Wiesel

The universe (which others call the Library) is composed of an indefinite and perhaps infinite number of hexagonal galleries, with vast air shafts between, surrounded by very low railings.

Jorge Luis Borges

Nothing contains all things. It is more precious than gold, without beginning and end, more joyous than the perception of bountiful light, more noble than the blood of kings, comparable to the heavens, higher than the stars, more powerful than a stroke of lightning, perfect and blessed in every way.

Otto von Guericke

What we do not know controls us.

Monica Ali

It's taken all my life to understand that it is not necessary to understand everything.

René Coty

Vice is perhaps a desire to learn everything.

Honoré de Balzac

. . . our senses, like our neighbors, hate what they do not understand.

Kahlil Gibran

Things are as bad and as good as they seem. There's no need to add anything extra.

Pema Chödrön

The void, it turns out, is alive.

Paul M. Sutter

Wherever I am / I am what is missing.

Mark Strand

Instant gratification takes too long.

Carrie Fisher

In French we say, *Je pense tellement pas au mal que je vois pas le mal.* "I'm so not thinking about harm that I don't see the harm."

Demna

It infuriates me to be wrong when I know I'm right.

Molière

And yet I knew better. I had known every second of every day that what I was doing was wrong and I had done it anyway.

Paul Harding

I think we all have a need to know what we do not need to know.

William Safire

Even his ignorance is encyclopedic.

Stanislaw J. Lec

Was this a test of faith? It affirmed only their faith in their ignorance.

Rumaan Alam

Most of the sighs we hear have been edited.

Stanislaw J. Lec

A man hears what he wants to hear and disregards the rest.

Paul Simon

Sometimes the smartest guy in the room is the one doing the dumbest things.

Dennis Brogan

So it's fine to be alone. So long as you have your distractions.

Rachel Kushner, "A King Alone"

We are well advised to keep on nodding terms with the people we used to be, whether we find them attractive company or not.

Joan Didion

You cannot unroll that snowball which is you: there is no "you" except your life — lived.

Jane Ellen Harrison

We're all in this alone.

Lily Tomlin

There must be more to life than having everything.

Maurice Sendak

Everything can change in an instant. Everything. And then there is only before and after.

Phyllis Reynolds Naylor

I just want to be dwarfed / by everything / these days.

Megan Fernandes

The vacuum is singing to us a harmony underlying reality itself.

Paul M. Sutter

Blood hunger / Has an endless stomach.

Joy Harjo, "An Ordinary Morning"

It was the kind of morning that the citizens of this island kingdom [England] very rarely saw: an established and adamant clarity, with the sun pinned into place, as firm as a gilt tack; and the sky, seemingly embarrassed by such exalted pressure, kept blushing an even deeper blue.

Martin Amis

Love commingled with hate is more powerful than love. Or hate.

Joyce Carol Oates

I don't think we don't love each other.

Harold Pinter

Hate has caused a lot of problems in the world but has yet to solve one yet.

Maya Angelou

All advice is first and foremost a reminder to myself.

Joel W. Jackson

Advice is what we ask for when we already know the answer but wish we didn't.

Erica Jong

A committee is an animal with four back legs.

John le Carré

. . . a smile that looked as though someone had plugged him in.

David Foster Wallace, *Something to Do with Paying Attention*

I have nothing to say and I am saying it and that is poetry.

John Cage

Poetry atrophies when it gets too far from music.

Ezra Pound

If I had a religion, it would be music, because I find it to be so rich, so universal, so profound.

Kaija Saariaho

I believe in all that has never yet been spoken.
Rainer Maria Rilke

Poetry makes nothing happen.
W. H. Auden

Poets think they're pitchers when they're really catchers.
Jack Spicer

Nothing is real.
John Lennon and Paul McCartney

When you got nothing, you got nothing to lose.
Bob Dylan

A poem should not mean / But be.
Archibald MacLeish

Honk if you wish all difficult poems were profound.
Ben Lerner

It's just a poem, not a platter of brains.
Chelsey Minnis

Poetry is what Milton saw when he went blind.
Don Marquis

If I read a book and it makes my whole body so cold no fire can ever warm me, I know that is poetry. If I feel physically as if the top of my head were taken off, I know that is poetry. These are the only ways I know it. Is there any other way?

Emily Dickinson, *Life and Letters of Emily Dickinson*, Martha Bianchi, ed.

The body says what words cannot.

Martha Graham

Having no destination, I am never lost.

Ikkyū

What happens is that almost nothing happens.

Anthony Lane

It's kind of fun to do the impossible.

Walt Disney

All speech is failed music.

Jameson Fitzpatrick

One way of looking at speech is to say that it is a constant stratagem to cover nakedness.

Harold Pinter

Never get a mime talking. He won't stop.

Marcel Marceau

Every conversation is a podcast if you close your eyes.

Karen Chee

Does every conversation with you have to be the director's cut?

Jonathan Lethem

Don't talk so much with your mouth.

Fran Ross

She possessed the majesty of plain speech.

Paul Harding

It can always get worse. Because when you hit rock bottom, you can still fall further into the abyss.

Tokyo, *Money Heist*

. . . everything hated everything else, and everything else, in return, hated everything back. Everything soft hated everything hard, and vice versa, cold fought heat, heat fought cold, everything honked and yelled and swore at everything, and all was weightless, and all hated weight.

Martin Amis

When you set off a bomb, you don't always know where the roof is going to cave in.

Amy Davidson Sorkin

Nobody is nothing.

Joseph O'Connor

Nobody knows how to feel and they're checking around for hints.

Don De Lillo

Nobody knows you. You are the neighbor of nothing.

Mark Strand

Nobody wants to be here and nobody wants to leave.

Cormac McCarthy

. . . a new origin story that keeps repeating. / It says: here, here, here. An eternal present that keeps loss at bay.

Megan Fernandes

Liars are always the loudest.

Jefferson Grieff, *Inside Man*

There is no one there to see it. The world is doing what it always does, demonstrating itself to itself.

Michael Cunningham

I like a view but I like to sit with my back turned to it.

Alice B. Toklas

Nothing in the world's more expensive than "free."

The Deacon, *The Wire*

What is bought is cheaper than a gift.

Miguel de Cervantes

Freedom lies across the field of the difficult conversation. And the more difficult the conversation, the greater the freedom

Shonda Rhimes

There is no home / and nothing to return to, just a series of shadows, partial signs of presence: a flickering.

Megan Fernandes

Nobody was ever murdered by a painting.

Joseph O'Connor

It is completely unimportant. That is why it is so interesting.

Agatha Christie

I don't want to see the uncut version of anything.

Jean Kerr

Any thinking person is afraid of what they deserve.

Jefferson Grieff, *Inside Man*

If I had to live my life again, I'd make the same mistakes, only sooner.

Tallulah Bankhead

There is a glory in a great mistake.

Nathalia Crane

Eliminate something superfluous from your life. Break a habit. Do something that makes you feel insecure.

Piero Ferrucci

Depend upon it, there is nothing so unnatural as the commonplace.

Arthur Conan Doyle

It is terrible to have the life of another person attached to our own like a bomb which we hold in our hands, unable to get rid of it without committing a crime.

Marcel Proust

Yield and you need not break.

Lao Tzu

Bend too far, you're already broken.

Cedric Daniels, *The Wire*

The photographer is always in the picture.

Joseph O'Connor

A photograph is a secret about a secret. The more it tells you, the less you know.

Diane Arbus

A man's most open actions have a secret side to them.

Joseph Conrad

The practice of deception was so constant with her that it got to be a kind of truth.

Louise Erdrich

Like any delicate creature, love depends on an ecosystem, a context.

Julia Glass

Let your children go if you want to keep them.

Malcolm Forbes

When I grow up I want to be a little boy.

Joseph Heller

When the heart speaks, the mind finds it indecent to object.

Milan Kundera

Only an American would write a play called *A Streetcar Named Desire*. An Englishman would entitle it *A Bus Called Passing Interest*.

Joseph O'Connor

He has this, at least — he has the finality of nothing happening.

Michael Cunningham

There is no intellectual exercise which is not ultimately useless.

Jorge Luis Borges

The greatest power available to man is not to use it.

Meister Eckhart

Never talk yourself out of knowing you're in love. . . or into thinking that you are.

Julia Glass

Where there's fear, that can turn into violence.

Sacha Baron Cohen

It is always the false that makes you suffer, the false desires and fears, the false values and ideas, the false relationships between people.

Sri Nisargadatta Maharaj

Respect is the ultimate currency.

Clive Owen, *Inside Man*

The fights you have are never about the thing you're fighting about. It's always about something else. It's about a story. It's about respect. It's about recognition, something deep.

Barack Obama

What if the story you are telling is racing against death?

Jiayang Fan

Life is a great surprise. I do not see why death should not be an even greater one.

Vladimir Nabokov

Abandon the false and you are free of pain; truth makes happy, truth liberates.

Sri Nisargadatta Maharaj

Doing the right thing is never the wrong thing.

Ted Lasso, *Ted Lasso*

We're all just walking each other home.

Ram Dass

4

WRITERS & WRITING, ETC.

Judging a book by its cover is one of the wisest judgments we can make.

Adam Gopnik

You can't judge a book by its cover, but you can by its first few chapters and most certainly by its last.

Raymond "Red" Reddington, *The Blacklist*

Many a good book has dark covers.

Agrippa Hull

Sometimes when you are in a dark place, you think you've been buried, but you actually have been planted.

Christine Cane

Gutenberg made everybody a reader. Xerox makes everybody a publisher.

Marshall McLuhan

The Medium Is the Message.

Marshall McLuhan

In high art and pure science detail is everything.

Vladimir Nabokov

Paradise / Is exactly like / Where you are right now / Only much much / Better.

Laurie Anderson

I have always imagined that Paradise will be a kind of library.

Jorge Luis Borges

— How do you know all this?
— I'm a fucking librarian.

Jenny Offill

Of course it's all right for librarians to smell of drink.

Barbara Pym

The America I loved still exists at the front desks of our public libraries.

Kurt Vonnegut Jr.

Why do writers write? Because it isn't there.

Thomas Berger

Definitions belong to the definers, not the defined.

Toni Morrison

When ideas fail, words come in very handy.

Johann Wolfgang von Goethe

It's only words, unless they're true.

David Mamet

That's all we have, finally, the words, and they had better be the right ones.

Raymond Carver

Sometimes a scream is better than a thesis.

Ralph Waldo Emerson

He who cannot howl / Will not find his pack.

Charles Simic

An artist will betray himself by some sort of sincerity.

G. K. Chesterton

Why don't you write books people can read?

Nora Joyce, to her husband, James

I think all writing is profoundly unmarried.

Elizabeth Hardwick

Art is I; science is we.

Claude Bernard

We are what we are.

Garrison Keillor, motto of Lake Wobegone

My favorite ethnic group is smart.

Dagoberto Gilb

Whatever they criticize you for, intensify it.

Jean Cocteau

Let me give you my feedback. My feedback is arf arf arf.

Chelsey Minnis

I'm quite illiterate, but I read a lot.

J. D. Salinger

One heartbreak can produce many novels. But you have to have a heart that can break.

Brian Morton

Books are where things are explained to you; life is where things aren't.

Julian Barnes

All publicity is good, except an obituary notice.

Brendan Behan

Publicity overrates everything.

George Balanchine

Writing is so difficult that I often feel that writers, having had their hell on earth, will escape all punishment hereafter.

Jessamyn West

If you can't annoy somebody . . . there's little point in writing.

Kingsley Amis

Be obscure clearly.

E. B. White

Remarks are not literature.

Gertrude Stein

I have made this [letter] longer than usual, only because I have not had the time to make it shorter. *Je n'ai fait celle-ci plus longue que parce que je n'ai pas eu le loisir de la faire plus courte.*

Blaise Pascal

A word is not a crystal, transparent and unchanged, it is the skin of a living thought and may vary greatly in color and content according to the circumstances and the time in which it is used.

Oliver Wendell Holmes Jr.

I think it pisses God off if you walk by the color purple in a field somewhere and don't notice it.

Alice Walker

Everyone knows that it is much harder to turn word into deed than deed into word.

Maxim Gorky

I love deadlines. I love the whooshing noise they make as they go by.

Douglas Adams

"I'm on deadline" can get you out of things . . . Whatever kind of work you do, it's always cooler to be on deadline.

Terry McDonell

All good writing is *swimming under water* and holding your breath.

F. Scott Fitzgerald

Personally I'm always ready to learn, although I do not always like being taught.

Winston Churchill

If it sounds like writing, I rewrite it.

Elmore Leonard

You already write *how* you write, just give in.

Grace E. Lavery

The object of art is to give life a shape.

Jean Anouilh

Not everything needs to be written and not everyone needs to write.

Grace E. Lavery

To ask the hard question is simple.

W. H. Auden

Simple can be harder than complex: You have to work hard to get your thinking clean to make it simple.

Steve Jobs

Success is a lousy teacher. It seduces smart people into thinking they can't lose.

Bill Gates

If you want to be true to life, start lying about it.

John Fowles

Poetry lies its way to the truth.

John Ciardi

Almost all poetry is a failure because it sounds like somebody saying, "Look, I have written a poem!"

Charles Bukowski

A poem points to nothing but itself.

E. M. Forster

I made up my mind that I would hold onto nothing, that I would expect nothing, that henceforth I would live as an animal, a beast of prey, a rover, a plunderer.

Henry Miller

You cannot pluck love out of your heart as you would pull a tooth.

Honoré de Balzac

In poetry, everything which must be said is almost impossible to say well.

Paul Valéry

Between what is said and not meant, and what is meant and not said, most of love is lost.

Khalil Gibran

My secrets cry aloud. / I have no need for tongue.

Theodore Roethke

The big secret in life is that there is no big secret.

Oprah Winfrey

The secret is this: strength lies solely in tenacity.

Louis Pasteur

My heart keeps open house, / My doors are widely swung.

Theodore Roethke

Look at the view.

Anna Quindlen

Exhaust the little moment. / Soon it dies.

Gwendolyn Brooks

It's so much easier to write a résumé than to craft a spirit.

Anna Quindlen

You choose to be a novelist, but you're chosen to be a poet. . . .You have to be willing to give something terribly intimate and secret of yourself to the world and not care . . .

May Sarton

Ultimately, despite my intention to plot my novel in detail before I began, I did the opposite: I wrote to discover the novel.

Abraham Verghese

Well, fuck the plot! That is for precocious schoolboys. What matters is the imaginative truth.

Edna O'Brien

Most of what matters in our lives takes place in our absence.

Salman Rushdie

The man is most original who can adapt from the greatest number of sources.

Thomas Carlyle

The main thing is to keep the main thing the main thing.

Stephen Covey

Obsessions are the only things that matter.

Patricia Highsmith

Everybody has a plan until they get hit.

Mike Tyson

When you assume negative intent, you're angry.

Indra Nooyi

Good fiction is made of that which is real.

Ralph Ellison

Fiction reveals truths that reality obscures.

Jessamyn West

The novelist says in words what cannot be said in words.

Ursula K. Le Guin

She didn't even ask me how I was, or maybe she asked but gave me no space to respond.

Elena Ferrante

First forget *inspiration*. Habit is more dependable.

Octavia E. Butler

I love being a writer. What I hate is the paperwork.

Peter De Vries

She loved to walk down the street with a book under her arm. It had the same significance for her as an elegant cane for a dandy a century ago.

Milan Kundera

Women were perceived to belong to the interior, to need protection outside. It was a long fight to win our place on the sidewalk, one we're still battling to this day.

Lauren Elkin, *Flâneuse: Women Walk the City in Paris, New York, Tokyo, Venice, and London*

I never walk with headphones because it takes away from the sounds and energy that're around me.

Brooke Porter Katz

I once read that [composer] Erik Satie frequently missed the last train from Paris in order to walk the several miles home, stopping under streetlights to jot down ideas.

Nick Tovarek

Almost always, going out for a walk makes me feel significantly better.

Corinna Wollmann

I always feel better after walking. If I've got nowhere to be, then I happily float from whim to whim.

Nick Tovarek

I wouldn't enjoy a walk that I planned. It's just like when you're traveling: You go to see something you haven't seen before, but you want to see something you didn't expect. The only way you get that is with spontaneity.

Dan Owen

You would think [aimless wandering] were easy, but it's not. We're so used to having an agenda, and we're so used to our minds being in charge. Aimless wandering requires that you put the mind in the back seat and follow other currents of your interior landscape; not just the current of the mind.

Laura Teusink

I know every book of mine by its smell, and I have but to put my nose between the pages to be reminded of all sorts of things.

George Gissing

It's rather disconcerting to realize that you can't take even a book with you.

Drue Heinz

Life passes into pages if it passes into anything.

James Salter

Write beautifully what people don't want to hear.

Frederick Seidel

Go to where the silence is and say something.

Amy Goodman

The use of language is all we have to pit against death and silence.

Joyce Carol Oates

Language alone protects us from the scariness of things with no names.

Toni Morrison

Language is a skin: I rub my language against the other.

Roland Barthes

Language is the house of Being.

Martin Heidegger

A really perfect poem has an infinitely small vocabulary.

Jack Spicer

He knew everything about literature except how to enjoy it.

Joseph Heller

The primary object of a student of literature is to be delighted.

Lord David Cecil

However you frame yourself as an artist, the frame is too small.

Rick Rubin

Why, after all, should readers never be harrowed? Surely there is enough happiness in life without having to go to books for it.

Dorothy Parker, attributed.

One can't build little white picket fences to keep nightmares out.

Anne Sexton

Painting is easy when you don't know how, but very difficult when you do.

Edgar Degas

My vocabulary is adequate for writing notes and keeping journals but absolutely useless for an active moral life.

Grace Paley

There's always something new by looking at the same thing over and over.

John Updike

Every artist has one story to tell — over and over and over and over and over and over again.

Bruce Springsteen

The world, the human world, is bound together not by protons and electrons, but by stories.

Brian Morton

We tell ourselves stories in order to live.

Joan Didion

I worry incessantly that I might be too clear.

Alan Greenspan

No one has a finer command of the language than the person who keeps his mouth shut.

Sam Rayburn

Discovering that one has nothing to say, one seeks a way to say *that*.

Susan Sontag

Languages for me have a secret venom that every so often foams up and for which there is no antidote.

Elena Ferrante

... languages eddy, their thorns snagging through / rain's arrhythmia. Misunderstanding, our common feast.

Cynthia Dewi Oka

There is no surer way to misread any document than to read it literally.

Learned Hand

But. There's always a "but" in life, isn't there?

Brian Morton

I've always made love and always written as if I were going to die afterwards. . . .

Annie Ernaux

You latch onto small details and from them write the book of your life.

Paul Lynch, *The Black Snow*

But I invent nothing; you just have to listen — the unspoken says more than the spoken.

Elena Ferrante

A word is a thought committed to air, / a wondering aloud, / a tireless seeking / without any answers.

Emma Sedlak

Let me keep my distance, always, from those who think they have the answers. Let me keep company always with those who say "Look!" and laugh in astonishment, and bow their heads.

Mary Oliver

It is better to know some of the questions than all of the answers.

James Thurber

If they can get you asking the wrong questions, they don't have to worry about the answers.

Thomas Pynchon

Questioning is the piety of thought.

Martin Heidegger

There ain't no answer. There ain't going to be any answer. There never has been an answer. That's the answer.

Gertrude Stein

show me someone not full of herself and i'll show you a hungry person

Nikki Giovanni

I have a simple philosophy. Fill what's empty. Empty what's full. Scratch where it itches.

Alice Roosevelt Longworth.

When you learn, teach. When you get, give.

Maya Angelou

Pretentious? *Moi*?

John Cleese

A flood of "ums" is like a continual cry for help by someone who can't help him- or herself.

Michael Erard

The longer you stay in one place, the greater your chances of disillusionment.

Art Spander

A divorce is like an amputation, you survive but there's less of you.

Margaret Atwood

A philosophical doctrine is in the beginning a seemingly true description of the universe; as the years pass it becomes a mere chapter — if not a paragraph or a noun — in the history of philosophy.

Jorge Luis Borges

History is not what's done. It's what gets into writing.

Meir Shalev

This matters, the remaking of an untenable world through the nib of a pen; it matters so much I can't stop doing it.

Carol Shields

Unlike stories, real life, when it has passed, inclines toward obscurity, not clarity.

Elena Ferrante

Imagination and fiction make up more than three quarters of our real life.

Simone Weil

He listened to himself as if it were someone else's tale he was telling.

Benjamin Black, *Elegy for April*

Our genealogies of bones / Are stacked in the graveyard, and live / In the stories we shared this morning.

Joy Harjo, "An Ordinary Morning"

I am for an art that takes its form from the lines of life itself, that twists and extends and accumulates and spits and drips, and is heavy and coarse and blunt and sweet and stupid as life itself.

Claes Oldenburg

Do not imagine that Art is something which is designed to give gentle uplift and self-confidence. Art is not a *brassière*.

Julian Barnes

Artists who seek perfection in everything are those who can attain it in nothing.

Eugène Delacroix

Language is the house of Being. In its home man dwells.

Martin Heidegger

There is no agony like bearing an untold story inside of you.

Maya Angelou

Whatever is on the outside can be taken away at any time. Only what is inside you is safe.

Jeanette Winterson

Real life has no clear trajectory or boundaries, and the great weakness of stories is their urge toward making clear and sharp what is not.

Christopher Warley

I am the exterminator. That mousetrap is called my pen.

Sandra Cisneros

All rabbit holes are dark. They're underground.

Sidonie Baker, *Slow Horses*

A great artist needs nothing but his woundedness.

Joseph O'Connor

Artists are the antennae of the race.

Ezra Pound

Trying is the first step towards failure.

Dan Greaney

Failure's contagious.

Jackson Lamb, *Slow Horses*

When you've been a writer for a long time, you develop an uncanny sensitivity to barely perceptible verbal signals of rejection.

Brian Morton

With all the intermingling of concepts, it was increasingly difficult to find a phrase of one's own, the kind that, when silently repeated, helped one live.

Annie Ernaux

. . . it's easier to lie / through the voice / than in the honesty of ink.

Emma Sedlak

Violence does not and cannot exist by itself; it is invariably intertwined with *the lie*.

Alexander Solzhenitsyn

I consider poetry a dialogue with myself, a conversation more private than a journal.

Sandra Cisneros

There is no such thing as conversation. It is an illusion. There are intersecting monologues, that is all.

Rebecca West

Storytelling reveals meaning without committing the error of defining it.

Hannah Arendt

To know yourself, you must sacrifice the illusion that you already do.

Vironika Tugaleva

The most dangerous of our calculations are those we call illusions.

Georges Bernanos

My job is to get your attention and keep it long enough for the message to get across.

David Lance Goines

I write what I think, but how do I know what I think till I write it down?

Sandra Cisneros

Operas are miracles, . . . How they come together, all those meticulous arts enfolded in one.

Julia Glass

Miracles are instantaneous, they cannot be summoned, but come of themselves, usually at unlikely moments and to those who least expect them.

Katherine Anne Porter

. . . as if everything I write comes to me by way of the heart, a muscle as strong as a python but as fragile as a lemon meringue pie.

Sandra Cisneros

Words aren't the only way / to tell stories.

Emma Sedlak

There are only two or three human stories, and they go on repeating themselves as fiercely as if they had never happened before.

Willa Cather

What do you do when you're no longer the hero of your own story?

Michael Cunningham

So little to say / So urgent / to say it

Leonard Cohen, "My Career"

The object isn't to make art, it's to be in that wonderful state which makes art inevitable.

Robert Henri

It's not unusual for science to catch up to art, eventually. Nor is it unusual for art to catch up to the spiritual.

Rick Rubin

This spiritual life, in the end it is not a choice, it's what's left when you run out of choices.

Russell Brand

Coincidences are spiritual puns.

G. K. Chesterton

Science without religion is lame, religion without science is blind.

Albert Einstein

Every day, poetry summons me in the same way that the minarets let loose their silk call to prayer.

Sandra Cisneros

Libraries are reservoirs of strength, grace, and wit, reminders of order, calm, and continuity, lakes of mental energy, neither warm nor cold, light nor dark. The pleasure they give is steady, unorgastic, reliable, deep, and long-lasting. In any library in the world, I am at home, unself-conscious, still, and absorbed.

Germaine Greer

The great writers of aphorisms read as if they had all known each other very well.

Elias Canetti

A book is a dream that you hold in your hands.

Neil Gaiman

Some sentences release their poison only after years.

Elias Canetti

Any day now, any day now / I shall be released.

Bob Dylan

Words are loaded pistols.

Jean-Paul Sartre

The covers of this book are too far apart.

Ambrose Bierce [One-sentence book review]

5

WIT & WISDOM

You can observe a lot by watchin'.

Yogi Berra

Reserving judgments is a matter of infinite hope.

F. Scott Fitzgerald

There are two ways to be fooled. One is to believe what isn't true; the other is to refuse to believe what is true.

Søren Kierkegaard

Where there is no belief, there is no blasphemy.

Salman Rushdie

. . . most of the difficult decisions in life don't involve right against wrong, but right against right.

Brian Morton

Luck is the residue of design.

Branch Rickey

We congratulate ourselves on having abandoned our vices, when it is they who have abandoned us.

Brian Morton

The golden rule is that there are no golden rules.

George Bernard Shaw

No generalization is wholly true — not even this one.

Oliver Wendell Holmes Jr.

Sacred cows make the tastiest hamburger.

Abbie Hoffman

When people are least sure they are most dogmatic.

John Kenneth Galbraith

Certainty generally is illusion.

Oliver Wendell Holmes Jr.

You can always count on a murderer for a fancy prose style.

Vladimir Nabokov

. . . the main element of his conversational style was knowingness; he had the style of connoisseurship.

Brian Morton

The only thing that makes life possible is permanent, intolerable uncertainty: not knowing what comes next.

Ursula K. Le Guin

Nothing is particularly hard if you divide it into small jobs.

Henry Ford

No question is so difficult to answer as that to which the answer is obvious.

George Bernard Shaw

The only difference between myself and a madman is that I am not mad.

Salvador Dalí

I was thinking that we all learn by experience, but some of us have to go to summer school.

Peter De Vries

Between God and Me there is no "Between."

Meister Eckhart

And if I asked you to name all the things that you love, how long would it take for you to name yourself?

Sana Dabbas

The more we value things, the less we value ourselves.

Bruce Lee

Here is God's purpose — / for God, to me, it seems, / is a verb / not a noun.

R. Buckminster Fuller

Dividing human differences into distinct illnesses is like dividing up the color spectrum into distinct colors.

Roy Richard Grinker, *Nobody's Normal*

Let there be spaces in your togetherness.

Kahlil Gibran

Everybody lies about sex.

Robert A. Heinlein

We must travel in the direction of our fear.

John Berryman

When you starts measuring somebody, measure him *right*, child, measure him right.

Lorraine Hansberry

Physical tiredness is a magnifying glass.

Elena Ferrante

Strength and wisdom are not opposing values.

Bill Clinton

I believe in compulsory cannibalism. If people were forced to eat what they killed there would be no war.

Abbie Hoffman

She authenticated the not-facts by simply repeating that they had happened.

Aldous Huxley

I was brought up to believe that the only thing worth doing was to add to the sum of accurate information in this world.

Margaret Mead

It is a far, far better thing to have a firm anchor in nonsense than to put out on the troubled seas of thought.

John Kenneth Galbraith

Find out before you flip out.

Ted Lasso, *Ted Lasso*

It is the final proof of God's omnipotence that he need not exist in order to save us.

Peter De Vries

Insanity is doing the same thing over and over again, but expecting different results.

Rita Mae Brown

A paranoid is someone who has all the facts.

William S. Burroughs

Facts do not cease to exist because they are ignored.

Aldous Huxley

The great tragedy of Science — the slaying of a beautiful hypothesis by an ugly fact.

Thomas Henry Huxley

Somebody always leaves a banana-skin on the scene of a tragedy.

Graham Greene

All our scientific and philosophic ideals are altars to unknown gods.

William James

Compassion is not a relationship between the healer and the wounded. It's a relationship between equals.

Pema Chödrön

Rarely, if ever, are any of us healed in isolation. Healing is an act of communion.

bell hooks

To forgive is to set a prisoner free and discover that the prisoner was you.

Lewis B. Smedes

There are no innocent bystanders. What are they doing there in the first place?

William S. Burroughs

In other countries poverty is a misfortune — with us it is a crime.

Edward George Bulwer-Lytton

To lead the people, walk behind them.

Lao-tzu

I should sooner live in a society governed by the first two thousand names in the Boston telephone directory than in a society governed by the two thousand faculty members of Harvard University.

William F. Buckley Jr.

Applause is the echo of a platitude.

Ambrose Bierce

What happens to the hole when the cheese is gone?

Bertolt Brecht

Life, friends, is boring. We must not say so.

John Berryman

If it doesn't cause any kind of reaction, it just doesn't exist.

Demna

The wickedness of the world is so great you have to run your legs off to avoid having them stolen from under you.

Bertolt Brecht

We become who we are.

Red Reddington, *The Blacklist*

We become what we do.

Madame Chiang Kai-shek

. . . there is only so much sourness sweetness can take without becoming bitter.

Paul Lynch, *The Black Snow*

Be kind whenever possible. It is always possible.

The Dalai Lama

Lucky people are not obliged to cultivate shrewdness.

Carol Shields

The best thing to do with the best things in life is to give them up.

Dorothy Day

The best things in life aren't things.

Ann Landers

Oh, oh I said, "I'm so happy I could die" / She said, "Drop dead," then left with another guy.

Elvis Costello

You can never get enough of what you don't need to make you happy.

Eric Hoffer

If you're not happy where you are, you won't be happy where you aren't.

Morton Kondracke

. . . a child never wants only what it's asking for, in fact a satisfied demand makes even more unbearable the need that has not been confessed.

Elena Ferrante

The less I needed, the better I felt.

Charles Bukowski

If you don't risk anything, you risk even more.

Erica Jong

When someone else's happiness is your happiness, that is love.

Lana Del Rey

Happiness lies not in finding what is missing, but in finding what is present.

Tara Brach

Happiness is a perfume you cannot pour on others without getting some on yourself.

Ralph Waldo Emerson

No human being can really understand another, and no one can arrange another's happiness.

Graham Greene

A dysfunctional family is any family with more than one person in it.

Mary Karr

She had spent her life half strangled by what-ifs.

Maggie O'Farrell, *The Vanishing Act of Esmé Lennox*

I sure did live in this world.

Toni Morrison

O world, I cannot hold thee close enough.

Edna St. Vincent Millay

[Race is] fundamentally a social category.

David Reich

What we want to be becomes what we think we are. Identity is aspirational.

Libby Copeland

You know, it's always amazed me how many perfectly intelligent people wish for things they already have.

Julia Glass

Time is the enemy of secret-keepers, because with time comes the inevitable revelation, one way or the other.

Libby Copeland

We have met the enemy and he is us.

Walt Kelly

A riot is at bottom the language of the unheard.

Martin Luther King Jr.

Once you know it, you can't un-know it.

Brianne Kirkpatrick

I learn by going where I have to go.

Theodore Roethke

The machine threatens all achievement.

Rainer Maria Rilke

. . . one opaque action generates others of increasingly pronounced opacity, and so the problem is to break the chain.

Elena Ferrante

To be faithful that way is to be profoundly unfaithful.

Robert Icke

Doubt the man who swears to his devotion.

Louise Colet

Love involves a peculiar unfathomable combination of understanding and misunderstanding.

Diane Arbus

What is the most beautiful in virile men is something feminine; what is most beautiful in feminine women is something masculine.

Susan Sontag

Every sense is graceful, an agent of grace: touch, smell, taste.

Hilary Mantel, *Learning to Talk*

When I don't touch you it's a mistake in any life, / in each place and forever.

Bob Hicok

Grace strikes us when we are in great pain and restlessness.

Paul Tillich

. . . actual heroism receives no ovation, entertains no one. No one queues up to see it. No one is interested.

David Foster Wallace, *Something to Do with Paying Attention*

Do what you can, with what you have, where you are.

Theodore Roosevelt

Depression is a cold of the heart.

Psycho Doctor, Japanese TV drama

Whispers are the sound of stigma.

Roy Richard Grinker

The concept of the normal is properly a variant of the concept of the good. It is that which society has approved.

Ruth Benedict

The truth you believe and cling to makes you unavailable to hear anything new.

Pema Chödrön

I was not going to know; I was not even going to know what *I* thought.

Laurie Colwin

Candor is the last resort of the tasteless.

Joseph O'Connor

There is less in this man than meets the eye.

Tallulah Bankhead

I have always found that the man whose second thoughts are good is worth watching.

J. M. Barrie

I have my faults, but changing my tune is not one of them.

Samuel Beckett

As our eyes grow accustomed to sight they armor themselves against wonder.

Leonard Cohen

It is strange that the eye can love what mind and body hate.

J. A. Baker

Bring me the sunset in a cup.

Emily Dickinson

I shut my eyes in order to see.

Paul Gauguin

We were surprised once, long ago; and now we can never be surprised again.

John Ashbery

The visionary is the only true realist.

Federico Fellini

To see, we must forget the name of the thing we are looking at.

Claude Monet

We never really see each other, we never say the things we should like to.

Marcel Proust

The nude is condemned to never being naked. Nudity is a form of dress.

John Berger

There is a degree of tolerance which borders on insult.

Jean Rostand

To overpraise is a subtle form of disrespect — and everybody knows it.

Mary Gaitskill

In certain trying circumstances . . . profanity furnishes a relief denied even to prayer.

Mark Twain

Be careful what you say. It comes true. It comes true.

Maxine Hong Kingston

War is fear cloaked in courage.

William C. Westmoreland

Don't play what's there, play what's not there.

Miles Davis

Sometimes you have to be silent to be heard.

Stanislaw J. Lec

The word "listen" contains the same letters as the word "silent."

Alfred Brendel

Violence is the repartee of the illiterate.

Alan Brien

Silence is the unbearable repartee.

G. K. Chesterton

Silence encourages the tormentor, never the tormented.

Elie Wiesel

Seek simplicity and distrust it.

Alfred North Whitehead

I don't seek, I find.

Pablo Picasso

First find, then search.

Jean Cocteau

The artist must say it without saying it.

Duke Ellington

Art teaches nothing, except the significance of life.

Henry Miller

I want to do with you what spring does with the cherry trees.

Pablo Neruda

A work of art has an author, and yet, when it is perfect, it has something which is essentially anonymous about it.

Simone Weil

Human life is but a series of footnotes to a vast obscure unfinished masterpiece.

Vladimir Nabokov

If it were better, it wouldn't be as good.

Brendan Gill

I used to not be able to work if there were dishes in the sink. Then I had a child and now I can work if there is a corpse in the sink.

Anne Lamott

I do more painting when I'm not painting.

Andrew Wyeth

No artist is pleased...There is only a queer dissatisfaction, a blessed unrest that keeps us marching and makes us more alive than the others.

Martha Graham

But most of the time what happens to people is other people.

Jefferson Grieff, *Inside Man*

Anger is not humanizing. It's a rehearsal for the performance that never arrives.

Carol Shields

Some people have an inborn buoyancy, an immunity to being held accountable.

Julia Glass

The priest had said grace was a gathering of candles waiting to be lit by the sinner.

Joseph O'Connor

All sins are attempts to fill voids.

Simone Weil

No one wins. One side just loses more slowly.

Prez, *The Wire*

This is what happens when you get up too late. . . . Other people make your plans.

Julia Glass

. . . the grief in that voice, it would make a glass eye weep.

Joseph O'Connor

Cracks can open in the most ordinary life and swallow anyone at all.

Jefferson Grieff, *Inside Man*

Aren't proofs of God, by their very intent, heretical?

Julia Glass

Life moves along like water, it's all connected as the source of the river is connected to the mouth and the ocean.

Alan Watts

Enlightenment is when a wave realizes that it is the ocean.

Thich Nhat Hanh

For fast-acting relief, try slowing down.

Lily Tomlin

If the other is unknowable, then the self is unknowable as well.

Laurie Colwin.

Life itself is the proper binge.

Julia Child

6

LIFE & DEATH, ETC.

Life is rather like a tin of sardines — we're all of us looking for the key.

Alan Bennett

It's about nothing, everything else is about something; this, it's about nothing.

Larry David

Your paintings are like my films — they're about nothing . . . with precision.

Michelangelo Antonioni (to Mark Rothko)

"What do you see?"
"Nothing."
"Recognize it?"

Douglas Adams

People who are in love suspect nothing or everything.
Honoré de Balzac

Empty space is never-wasted space.
Andy Warhol

Miraculously unprepared / For the long littleness of life.
Frances Cornford

Breathless, we flung us on the windy hill, / Laughed in the sun, and kissed the lovely grass.
Rupert Brooke

We see the brightness of a new page where everything yet can happen.
Rainer Maria Rilke

I understand everything and everyone, and I am nobody and nothing.
George Bernard Shaw

Nobody, nobody is good enough.
Joseph Conrad

Where all, or almost all, are guilty, nobody is.
Hannah Arendt

. . . to exist is to drink oneself without thirst.
Annie Ernaux

... what do we really thirst for, / And how should we look for it, and where?

Carl Dennis

Everyone who is born holds dual citizenship, in the kingdom of the well and in the kingdom of the sick.

Susan Sontag

We cry for help, as humans do — / Before the truth, and after.

Leonard Cohen

To cure the body you must heal the mind.

Nepali proverb

Girls will be boys and boys will be girls / It's a mixed up, muddled up, shook up world except for Lola.

Ray Davies

Sex. In America an obsession. In other parts of the world a fact.

Marlene Dietrich

If I make this mistake again, I want this to be my mistake.

Robert King

If you can't be free, be a mystery.

Rita Dove

I too, sing America.

Langston Hughes

A policeman's job is only easy in a police state.

Orson Welles [spoken by Charlton
Heston in *Touch of Evil*]

The Discreet Charm of the Bourgeosie

Luis Buñuel

We live in a terrifying world, and fashion is a reflection of that.

Demna

Human existence is so fragile a thing and exposed to such dangers that I cannot love without trembling.

Simone Weil

She wanted her leaving to be an exclamation mark. She wanted her life to be an exclamation mark.

Brian Morton

The object of our technology is to control the world, to have a superelectronic pushbutton universe, where we can get anything we want, fulfill any desires simply by pushing a button.

Alan Watts

So if our technology were to succeed completely, and everything were to be under our control, we should eventually say, "We need a new button."

Alan Watts

Why do the world's shadows / come so close / as its wonders beckon?

Henri Cole, "Figs"

He not busy being born / Is busy dying.

Bob Dylan

You have this idea of I need to get there, but then you find out "there" keeps moving.

Jason Segel

Needing to know the answer is an addiction. The truth actually is in the silence. People are afraid to have a silent moment. Silence is all the truth and all the wisdom in the world.

Garry Shandling

Addiction is a grotesque exaggeration of the ordinary.

Russell Brand

Treat every moment as your last. It is not preparation for something else.

Shunryu Suzuki

Sometimes I would rather that people take years from my life than take away a moment.

Pearl Bailey

We do not remember days, we remember moments.

Cesare Pavese

There is no enlightenment outside of daily life.

Thich Nhat Hanh

My mother said, "When you grow up, not everybody is going to like you," and I said, "I need names." Now I have the list. I know who they are. You can just Google.

Bob Saget

Lists are a form of cultural hysteria.

Don De Lillo

Lists are a form of power.

A. S. Byatt

My favorite quote, and I'm really into quotes that I don't know who said them, this one quote kind of changed my life. "Comparison is the worst form of violence against yourself."

Whitney Cummings

Well, I'm sure getting better than I was, which is better than getting worse.

Garry Shandling

The more you do something, the more you lose fear.

Barack Obama.

Something froze there, and I think I'm constantly looking back on it. ...I don't think that goes away. I wouldn't want it to go away.

Jack Antonoff

Birth was the death of him.

Samuel Beckett

It's not that I'm afraid to die. I just don't want to be there when it happens.

Woody Allen

I was afraid I was goin to die and then I was afraid I wasnt.

Cormac McCarthy

Death must take me for someone else.

Samuel Beckett

We have no reliable guarantee that the afterlife will be any less exasperating than this one, have we?

Noël Coward

Live every minute as if you are late for the last train.

Colson Whitehead

Everyone's journey to the bottom is different.

Marc Maron

And though I am with autumn, my ears still echo the songs of spring.

Kahlil Gibran

Age only matters when one is aging.

Pablo Picasso

When we are too young our judgment is at fault; so also when we are too old.

Blaise Pascal

Old age . . . It's the only disease you don't look forward to being cured of.

Orson Welles

There's nothing more annoying than an old person who makes lame jests about his age.

Brian Morton

As you get older, you realize that there are more and more people that annoy you. So your world keeps narrowing, and getting narrower.

Rob Reiner

An old man in love is like a flower in winter.

Portuguese proverb

I will never be an old man. To me, old age is always fifteen years older than I am.

Bernard Baruch

Ah, but I was so much older then, I'm younger than that now.

Bob Dylan

Youth is given. One must put it away / like a doll in a closet, / take it out and play with it only / on holidays.

May Swenson

Time held me green and dying / Though I sang in my chains like the sea.

Dylan Thomas

On the stage it is always now.

Thornton Wilder

As a white candle / In a holy place, / So is the beauty / Of an agèd face.

Joseph Campbell

Alas, after a certain age every man is responsible for his face.

Albert Camus

The older you get, the harder it is to be concise. It's no longer adequate merely to say what you know; it's urgent to explain *how* you came to know it.

Brian Morton

Illness is the doctor to whom we pay most heed: to kindness, to knowledge we make promises only; pain we obey.

Marcel Proust

. . . the bruise eventually undoes itself, if somewhere a kindness / still counts as anything . . .

Carl Phillips

God is a concept / By which we measure / Our pain.

John Lennon

. . . death is an invisible presence all around us. We just pass through. None of us know how close we stand to it.

Paul Lynch, *The Black Snow*

I guess I just process death differently than some folks. Realizing you're not going to see that person again is always the most difficult part about it. But that feeling settles, and then you are glad you had that person in your life, and then the happiness and the sadness get all swirled up inside you.

John Prine

. . . what dreams are going to show up after we have fallen off the end of the universe?

Robert Icke

Dreams are — with extreme violence — the revealers of our times and our lives.

Salvador Dali

What is it that breathes fire into the equations and makes a universe for them to describe?

Stephen Hawking

Enduring tedium over real time in a confined space is what real courage is.

David Foster Wallace, *Something to Do with Paying Attention*

Mind what you love. For that matter, mind how you are loved.

Julia Glass

Were all men separated from their children and wives by an invisible ribbon of cluelessness?

Gary Shteyngart

Hope is kind of like dominoes: once one falls, the rest go down.

Tokyo, *Money Heist*

The audacity of hope! In the end, that is God's greatest gift to us.

Barack Obama

The difference between hope and despair is a different way of telling stories from the same facts.

Alain de Botton

Facts are subversive.

I. F. Stone

Facts are counterrevolutionary.

Eric Hoffer

The fact is a wire through which one sends a current.

Saul Bellow

Take closer care of your inner stories. They create your outer life.

Jaiya John

Old age is the most unexpected of all the things that can happen to a man.

Leon Trotsky

When people tell you how young you look, they are telling you how old you are.

Cary Grant

I'm now at the age where I've got to prove that I'm just as good as I never was.

Rex Harrison

Death alone is reliable.

Cristina García

The truth that many people never understand, until it is too late, is that the more you try to avoid suffering the more you suffer.

Thomas Merton

No one is safe from the worst that they can do.

Jefferson Grieff, *Inside Man*

We were resurrected ahead of time.

Annie Ernaux

Time is the longest distance between two places.

Tennessee Williams

I'm way too old to have this much of nothing.

Judd Altman, *This Is Where I Leave You*

Maybe the dead don't understand that they're dead.

Michael Cunningham

Don't grieve for the dead: they know what they're doing.

Clarice Lispector

... everyone dies alone, no matter how many people are in the room.

Julia Glass

We have all been in rooms / We cannot die in.

James Dickey

Men at forty / Learn to close softly / The doors to rooms they will not be / Coming back to.

Donald Justice

This is the way the world ends / This is the way the world ends / This is the way the world ends / Not with a bang but a whimper.

T. S. Eliot

The universe never explains why.

Rick Rubin

Go away. I'm all right.

H. G. Wells (last words)

A Note on Sources

By far I plucked most of the quotations from dog-eared pages of books sitting on my shelves. My morning habit of reading *The New Yorker* yielded tasty morsels. So did snippets of quotations I have collected over the years from things I have read, seen, or heard. Sources I mined for this effort included: *Garner's Quotations: A Modern Miscellany*, by Dwight Garner; *The Yale Book of Quotations*, edited by Fred R. Shapiro; *They Never Said It: A Book of Fake Quotes, Misquotes, & Misleading Attributions*, by Paul F. Boller Jr. and John George; *The Quote Verifier: Who Said What, Where, and When*, by Ralph Keyes; *Other People's Words: Wisdom for an Inspired and Productive Life*, by Seth M. Siegel; *Waiting for the Punch: Words to Live By from the WTF Podcast*, by Mark Maron and Brendan McDonald; *Bartlett's Familiar Quotations*, Eighteenth Edition, Geoffrey O'Brien, General Editor; *You Don't Have to Be Buddhist to Know Nothing: An Illustrious Collection of Thoughts on Naught*, conceived and edited by Joan Konner; *The 2,548 Best Things Anybody Ever Said*, selected and compiled by Robert Byrne; *The Art of Flaneuring: How to Wander with Intention and Discover a Better Life*, by Erika Owen; *Mentors: How to Help and Be Helped*, by Russell Brand; *I Really Needed This Today: Words to Live By*, by Hoda Kotb with Jane Lorenzini; *This Just Speaks to Me: Words to Live By*, by Hoda Kotb with Jane Lorenzini; *A Short Guide to a Happy Life*, by Anna Quindlen; *Honoré de Balzac: Epigrams on Men, Women, and Love*; *Be Where Your Feet Are: Seven Principles to Keep You Present, Grounded, and Thriving*, by Scot M. O'Neil, with Randal A. Wright and Michele Bender; *The Penguin Dictionary of Modern Quotations*, compiled by J. M. and M. J. Cohen; *Open Letter to Salvador Dali*, by Salvador Dali, translated by Harold J. Salemson; *The Unspeakable Confessions of Salvador Dali*, as told to André Parinaud; and *Literary Hub* (LitHub) digital newsletter.

About the Editor

In addition to compiling quotations, Paul Kocak has written critically acclaimed works of sports history, fiction, essays, poetry, memoir, and travel writing.

Made in the USA
Monee, IL
10 July 2023

38671412R00069